The Goats in the Turnip Field

Retold by Beverley Randell
Illustrated by Isabel Lowe

Once upon a time,
a boy was taking his goats home
along a road.

When the goats
saw a field of turnips,
they jumped over the gate.

The boy tried to chase them
out of the field.

But they would not go.

So the boy sat down and cried.

Rabbit came along.
"Why are you crying?" he asked.

The boy said, "I'm crying
because I can't chase the goats
out of the turnip field."

"I'll chase them out," said Rabbit.

But the goats would not go.

So Rabbit sat down and cried, too.

Fox came along.
"Why are you crying?"
he asked Rabbit.

Rabbit said, "I'm crying
because the boy is crying.
He is crying
because he can't chase the goats
out of the turnip field."

"I'll chase them out," said Fox.

But the goats would not go.

So Fox sat down and cried, too.

Wolf came along.
"Why are you crying?"
he asked Fox.

Fox said, "I'm crying
because Rabbit is crying."

"Rabbit is crying
because the boy is crying.
He is crying
because he can't chase the goats
out of the turnip field," said Fox.

"I'll chase them out," said Wolf.

But the goats would not go.

So Wolf sat down and cried, too.

A little bee came along.
"Why are you crying?"
she asked Wolf.

Wolf said, "I'm crying
because Fox is crying.
Fox is crying
because Rabbit is crying."

"Rabbit is crying
because the boy is crying.
And he is crying
because he can't chase the goats
out of the turnip field," said Wolf.

"I can do that,"
said the little bee.

Wolf and Fox and Rabbit
and the boy
laughed at the bee.

"**You** can't chase the goats
out of the turnip field,"
they said.
"You are too little."

"Watch me," said the bee,
and it flew to the goats
and buzzed in their ears.

The goats all ran out
of the turnip field!

And the boy
took them home at last.